CW00336865

HOW TO DRINK
WINE
OUT OF FISH HEADS
WHILE COOKING
LOBSTER
IN A VOLKSWAGEN
HUB CAP

ZIGGY ZEN
EASY SEAFOOD
RECIPES

MANY FISH TOGETHER
ARE KNOWN AS A SCHOOL.
CLEARLY THIS IS NOT
A SCHOOL.

SERIES EDITOR: SIMON MELHUISH
DESIGN & ILLUSTRATION: ROBYN RAWLINGS
EDITOR: AMY BREM-WILSON

PUBLISHED IN 2017 BY THE LAGOON GROUP,
PO BOX 58528, LONDON, SW13 3AY
ISBN: 978-1902813936

www.thelagoongroup.com

FIRST PUBLISHED IN AUSTRALIA IN 1998
BY PAN MACMILLAN AUSTRALIA PTY LIMITED
COPYRIGHT © 1998 BILLY BLUE MERCHANDISING PTY LTD
RECIPES BY HELEN TRACEY AND LINDA KAPLAN
ADDITIONAL WRITING BY ROSS RENWICK
SUPERVISING CHEFS MATT BLUNDELL AND GAVIN CUMMINS
OF KENTRA DOUBLE BAY AUSTRALIA
MANAGING DIRECTOR: AARON KAPLAN
CREATIVE DIRECTOR: ROSS RENWICK

LAGOON WOMAN TESTED

11   **LONELY ISLANDS**
GRILLED LOBSTER TAILS

14   **MALIBU DREAMING**
WHITING IN LIME AND PASSIONFRUIT SAUCE

16   **SLOW WHITE CLOUD**
FISH STOCK

17   **SONG OF SIAM**
SPICY THAI FISH SOUP

18   **BONDI MOON**
SMOKED OYSTER SOUP

19   **PEPPERCORN SUNRISE**
MUSSELS WITH FENNEL

20   **RIVER TREE**
SHELLFISH AND AVOCADO SOUP

21   **BLUE RAIN FALLING**
FISH SANDWICH

22   **MOON SEA MAN WOMAN**
COD CHOWDER

24   **KOSCIUSZKO WITH ORANGE SKY**
PRAWN MYSTERY

26   **GREEN FISH JUMPING**
WARM BALSAMIC FISH SALAD

28   **PINK SEA RISING**
FISH STEW

29   **CYCLONE ERNIE**
FISH PARCELS

32   **WARM DARWIN DAYS**
TANGY FISH FILLETS

33   **BLUE PACIFIC NOON**
GRILLED ATLANTIC SALMON CUTLETS

34   **BUTTERNUT BLUE**
CRISP PRAWN SALAD

BUYING THE BEST FISH.
WHAT TO LOOK FOR:

NICE PERSONALITY

INDEPENDENT INCOME

NORMAL SEXUAL HABITS (OR OTHER IF PREFERRED)

AVOID FISH THAT HAVE BEEN WRITTEN ON

ALSO LOOK FOR:

BRIGHT EYES WHICH PROTRUDE

CLEAN, FRESH SMELL

BRIGHT SPOTS AND MARKING

FIRM FINS

SHINY SCALES

WARM SMILE

ET TU FLATHEAD

LURES ARE OBJECTS WHICH YOU PUT ON YOUR FISHING LINE INSTEAD OF BAIT.

THEY ARE DECEPTIVELY DESIGNED TO MAKE FISH THINK THAT IT'S REGULAR FOOD.

LURES COME IN PRESSURE-PACKED CARDS WITH OPTIMISTIC ADVERTISING COPY.

HOWEVER, I'M HERE TO TELL YOU THAT THE FISH DON'T BELIEVE THE COPY.

WHEN YOU DECIDE TO USE LURES INSTEAD OF BAIT, YOU'RE ALREADY ON THE WAY TO A BETTER LIFE.

WHY? BECAUSE YOU DON'T HAVE TO FOOL AROUND WITH DIRTY, STINKING BAIT.

PUT THE LURE ON YOUR FISHING LINE AND CAST IT INTO PROMISING WATERS. (FOR A DEFINITION OF PROMISING WATERS REFER TO OTHER SOURCES.)

THE WHOLE AFFAIR WORKS BETTER IF YOU CAST THE LURE AND THEN DRINK A SMALL GLASS OF VERY FINE ENGLISH SHERRY AS YOU PULL IT IN.

HOW, YOU MAY ASK, CAN I DRINK A GLASS OF SHERRY WHILE HOLDING THE ROD WITH ONE HAND AND WINDING IN THE LURE WITH THE OTHER? EASY, I ANSWER. BY MAKING A STRUCTURE FROM A METAL COAT HANGER THAT FITS AROUND YOUR HEAD AND HOLDS A SHERRY GLASS TO YOUR LIPS.

I HAVE BEEN FISHING WITH LURES FOR FIFTEEN
YEARS AND HAVE NEVER CAUGHT A SINGLE FISH.
I HAVEN'T EVEN HAD A BITE. BUT I HAVE DRUNK
SOME VERY FINE SHERRY AND SPENT MANY
BEAUTIFUL AFTERNOONS OUTDOORS.

SO THE MAIN ADVANTAGE OF LURE FISHING
IS THAT YOU PROBABLY WON'T HAVE ANY
DEALINGS WITH LIVE FISH. WITHIN REASON I CAN
GUARANTEE IT.

I HAVE NOW TOLD YOU HOW TO HAVE A PERFECT
FISHING LIFE. WITHOUT BAIT. WITHOUT FISH. WITH
SHERRY. OR THE CORDIAL OF YOUR CHOICE.

THERE IS ONLY ONE RULE. BUY WHAT YOU NEED
FROM THE FISH SHOP.

UNEXPLAINED DOG

UNEXPLAINED TREE
(UNEXPLAINED COWGIRLS
MAY OCCUR)

LONELY ISLANDS
GRILLED LOBSTER TAILS

SERVES 4

I WANT TO TELL YOU ABOUT MY ATTITUDE TO DRINKING.

IT ISN'T REALLY AN ATTITUDE. IT'S JUST ONE OF THE THINGS THAT HAPPENS BEYOND MY CONTROL.

IN THE INTRODUCTION SPEECH TO THIS SMALL VOLUME CALLED ET TU FLATHEAD, I MENTIONED A STRUCTURE MADE FROM A WIRE COAT HANGER THAT HOLDS A GLASS OF FINE ENGLISH SHERRY TO YOUR LIPS.

I EXPECT, BY NOW, YOU HAVE MADE ONE AND HAVE DISCOVERED THAT THE USE OF FOAM RUBBER MAKES THE GRIP ON YOUR HEAD AND ON THE SHERRY GLASS A LITTLE EASIER.

AND YOU MAY HAVE ALSO DISCOVERED THAT IT'S QUITE A HANDY STRUCTURE, AS IT LEAVES BOTH HANDS FREE TO GET ON WITH LIFE'S WORK.

FORGIVE ME, BUT YOU HAVE PROBABLY ALSO DISCOVERED HOW DIFFICULT IT IS TO REFILL A GLASS THAT IS SO CLOSE TO YOUR CHIN, UNLESS YOU ARE EXTRAORDINARILY SHORT-SIGHTED.

I AM WORKING ON A REFILLING DEVICE, SOMETHING LIKE A MEDICAL DRIP THAT, ATTACHED TO A CRANE-LIKE STRUCTURE WHICH IN TURN IS ATTACHED TO THE SHERRY GLASS RIG.

IT IS A LESS THAN MINIMALIST SOLUTION, SO WHILE I SIMPLIFY IT, DO THE BEST YOU CAN WITH THE RIG YOU HAVE.

I WAS ABOUT TO TELL YOU ABOUT MY ATTITUDE TO DRINKING. I DON'T DRINK OFTEN. BUT WHEN I COOK, I DRINK.

SOME SAY THIS IS UNJUSTIFIABLY DANGEROUS, BUT IT'S NOT AS DANGEROUS AS DRIVING A TRAIN WHEN DRINKING...OR DECIDING YOU MIGHT LIKE TO GET MARRIED WHILE DRINKING.

I DON'T QUITE KNOW WHERE I'M GOING WITH THIS. FOR EXAMPLE, WHEN I'M COOKING MALIBU DREAMING, IT IS TWO GLASSES OF A NICE LITTLE CHARDONNAY FROM AUSTRALIA CALLED POET'S PILES AT ABOUT $2,300 A BOTTLE.

COOK IT AGAIN SAM IS TWO GLASSES OF A WHITE RUM MIXED WITH COCONUT MILK AND LIMES. A NASTY LITTLE DRINK INDEED.

I PRESENT TO YOU LONELY ISLANDS GRILLED LOBSTER TAILS. I WOULD THINK THAT THE COOKING TIME IS ABOUT THREE GLASSES OF A NICE CANARY FROM THE SOUTH-EAST CORNER OF SPAIN.

SUCCESSFUL FISH SHOP

4 GREEN LOBSTER TAILS
125ml/½ CUP MELTED BUTTER
3 TABLESPOONS LEMON JUICE
SALT AND PEPPER
CHOPPED PARSLEY
CHOPPED GARLIC

SLIT UNDERSIDE OF LOBSTER TAILS ONCE OR TWICE WITH A SHARP KNIFE.

PLACE UNDER GRILL, SHELL SIDE UP.

COOK UNTIL RED.

TURN OVER, RETURN TO GRILL, BASTING OFTEN WITH LEMON JUICE, MELTED BUTTER AND GARLIC.

COOK UNTIL MEAT IS TENDER AND WHITE.

SEASON WITH SALT, PEPPER AND PARSLEY.

VARIATION: HEAT OVEN TO 180°C/350°F/GAS MARK 4, PUT TAILS ON OVEN TRAY, BAKE FOR 15-20 MINUTES, DEPENDING ON SIZE.

SQUEEZE LEMON JUICE OVER AND SPRINKLE WITH PEPPER.

MALIBU DREAMING
WHITING IN LIME AND PASSIONFRUIT SAUCE

SERVES 4

I LIVE IN A PLACE WHICH HAS A BEACH AND A PORT AND A MODICUM OF CHARM, BUT NOT MUCH CHANCE OF A GREAT CAPPUCCINO.

AT THE NORTH END OF THE BEACH, THERE'S A NICE SURFING WAVE WHEN THE NORTH-EASTERS BEGIN BLOWING IN SPRING. THE WAVE RUNS ACROSS A REEF OF BOULDERS EDGED BY BRIGHT GREEN SEAGRASS AND IF YOU'RE CRUISING THROUGH THAT LITTLE PICTURE ON YOUR MALIBU SURFBOARD, YOU EVENTUALLY RUN ONTO A SAND BOTTOM.

AND THERE YOU SEE THEM, OR AT LEAST YOU SEE THEIR SHADOWS BECAUSE THEIR BODIES ARE SO TRANSPARENT...THE NEW SEASON'S WHITING. ONE OF THE WORLD'S GREAT EATING FISH.

BUT IF YOU'RE NOT CRUISING THROUGH THE CLEAR BRIGHT GREEN SPRING WATER AT AVALON ON YOUR ELEGANT SURFBOARD, YOU CAN SEE THEM AT THE FISH SHOP.

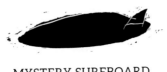

MYSTERY SURFBOARD

500g/1lb WHITING FILLETS
60ML/¼ CUP VERMOUTH
80ml/⅓ CUP FRESH LIME JUICE
5 TABLESPOONS FRESH
PASSIONFRUIT PULP
¼ TEASPOON SUGAR
SALT

POUR VERMOUTH AND JUICE OVER FISH AND SIMMER UNTIL FLESH FLAKES.

REMOVE TO WARM PLATTER AND KEEP WARM.

TO PAN JUICES, ADD PASSIONFRUIT PULP, SUGAR AND SALT TO TASTE.

HEAT SAUCE UNTIL HOT.

POUR OVER FISH TO SERVE.

SLOW WHITE CLOUD
FISH STOCK

3 FISH SKELETONS, INCLUDING SCALED FISH HEADS AND TRIMMINGS AND PRAWN SHELLS, ETC (IF THAT'S TOO TECHNICAL, THROW IN A COUPLE OF FISH CUTLETS OR SMALL SCALED FISH)

WATER, 1 TEASPOON SALT, 1 BAY LEAF, 2 SLICES LEMON, 1 STICK OF CELERY, 1 ONION (CHOPPED), 1 CARROT (CHOPPED), SPRIG OF PARSLEY, 3 BLACK PEPPERCORNS

WASH FISH PIECES THOROUGHLY.

PUT IN HEAVY SAUCEPAN.

ADD SALT, PEPPERCORNS, LEMON, BAY LEAF, WATER AND VEGETABLES.

BRING TO BOIL AND SIMMER FOR APPROXIMATELY 1 HOUR.

STRAIN STOCK CAREFULLY THROUGH A FINE STRAINER.

WHEN COLD, REFRIGERATE.

KEEPS FOR TWO DAYS, FREEZE IF NEEDED LATER.

SONG OF SIAM
SPICY THAI FISH SOUP

SERVES 4

1 LITRE/1¾ PINTS CLEAR CHICKEN STOCK (FROM THE DELI)

1 TABLESPOON THAI FISH SAUCE

2 TABLESPOONS FRESH LIME OR LEMON JUICE

5 STALKS LEMON GRASS

1½ TEASPOONS RED CURRY PASTE

400g/14oz MIXED FRESH FISH, CUBED

8 FRESH PRAWNS, PEELED AND DEVEINED

12 BUTTON MUSHROOMS

FRESH CORIANDER, CHOPPED

4 FRESH CHILLIES, SEEDED AND SLICED

BRING STOCK TO BOIL.

ADD FISH SAUCE, LIME OR LEMON JUICE, LEMON GRASS, CURRY PASTE AND CHILLIES.

BRING TO BOIL.

TASTE FOR SPICINESS.

ADD FISH, PRAWNS AND MUSHROOMS.

SIMMER UNTIL FISH COOKED.

REMOVE LEMON GRASS.

SERVE SPRINKLED WITH CORIANDER.

BONDI MOON
SMOKED OYSTER SOUP

SERVES 4

2 DESSERTSPOONS BUTTER
35g/¼ CUP PLAIN FLOUR
750ml/3 CUPS FISH STOCK
(YOU COULD USE WATER)
250ml/1 CUP MILK
1 OR 2 CANS SMOKED OYSTERS,
DRAINED AND CHOPPED
PINCH GROUND NUTMEG
SALT AND PEPPER
1 TEASPOON ANCHOVY SAUCE
¼ TEASPOON LEMON JUICE
CHOPPED PARSLEY OR CHIVES
SOUR CREAM (OPTIONAL)

MELT BUTTER IN SAUCEPAN.

STIR IN FLOUR AND COOK, STIRRING CONSTANTLY, UNTIL FROTHY.

GRADUALLY ADD STOCK AND MILK, STILL STIRRING CONSTANTLY.

COOK FOR 5 MINUTES, UNTIL MIXTURE THICKENS.

SEASON WITH SALT, PEPPER AND NUTMEG TO TASTE.

STIR IN OYSTERS, LEMON JUICE AND ANCHOVY SAUCE.

SERVE GARNISHED WITH PARSLEY OR CHIVES AND PERHAPS A DOLLOP OF SOUR CREAM.

PEPPERCORN SUNRISE
MUSSELS WITH FENNEL

SERVES 4-6

3kg/6½lb MUSSELS
375ml/1½ CUPS CLARET
2 CLOVES GARLIC, CUT IN HALF
SEVERAL PARSLEY SPRIGS
½ TEASPOON BLACK PEPPERCORNS
SALT TO TASTE
1 HEAD OF FENNEL, FINELY CHOPPED
2 BAY LEAVES
10 BASIL LEAVES, TORN

BRING EVERYTHING EXCEPT MUSSELS TO BOIL IN LARGE SAUCEPAN.

SCRUB MUSSELS AND REMOVE BEARDS.

ADD AS MANY AS YOU CAN TO SAUCEPAN AND COOK UNTIL OPEN.

REMOVE, THEN COOK REMAINDER.

DISCARD ANY UNOPENED SHELLS (THEY MAY BE BAD).

SERVE SHELLS IN GENEROUS-SIZED BOWLS WITH STRAINED STOCK POURED OVER THEM.

RIVER TREE
SHELLFISH AND AVOCADO SOUP

SERVES 4

1 TABLESPOON MELTED BUTTER

2 RIPE AVOCADOS

500ml/2 CUPS CHICKEN STOCK, OR 1 STOCK CUBE AND WATER

500ml/1 CUP CREAM (OR ½ CREAM AND MILK)

2 TABLESPOONS SHERRY

SALT AND PEPPER

ABOUT 350g/12oz COOKED SHELLFISH - SCALLOPS, MUSSELS, CLAMS, CRABMEAT. INCLUDE PRAWNS IF DESIRED

IN BLENDER, COMBINE ALL INGREDIENTS EXCEPT SHELLFISH.

BLEND UNTIL AVOCADO IS CREAMY.

PEEL AND DEVEIN PRAWNS.

LEAVE CLAMS AND MUSSELS IN SHELLS.

ADD SHELLFISH TO AVOCADO MIXTURE.

HEAT GRADUALLY, STIRRING CONSTANTLY.

SERVE HOT OR COLD.

BLUE RAIN FALLING
FISH SANDWICH

SERVES 4

2 STICKS CRISP CELERY, FINELY CHOPPED

1 TABLESPOON MAYONNAISE

PINCH OF PAPRIKA

1 TEASPOON CHOPPED BASIL

1 TEASPOON CHOPPED DILL

450g/2 CUPS COOKED, BONED, FLAKED FISH

SALT AND PEPPER

SMALL FRENCH LOAF, SLICED HORIZONTALLY AND BUTTERED

COMBINE CELERY, MAYONNAISE, PAPRIKA, BASIL, DILL, FISH, SALT AND PEPPER IN BLENDER (OR MIX WELL IN BASIN OR JAR).

SPREAD MIXTURE ON BREAD HALVES AND JOIN TOGETHER.

CAN BE WARMED IN OVEN BEFORE SERVING.

GOOD AT A PICNIC OR FOR A WEEKEND LUNCH.

MOON SEA MAN WOMAN
COD CHOWDER

SERVES 4-6

125g/4oz BACON, DICED
1 MEDIUM ONION, CHOPPED
½ CAPSICUM, FINELY CHOPPED
450g/1lb FILLET OF COD
310ml/1¼ CUP FISH STOCK (OPTIONAL)
2 MEDIUM POTATOES, DICED
BLACK PEPPER
500ml/¾-1 PINT MILK
PAPRIKA, CHIVES OR PARSLEY FOR GARNISH
1 DESSERTSPOON TURMERIC (OPTIONAL)

SAUTE BACON AND ONION IN MEDIUM SAUCEPAN UNTIL BACON IS CRISP.

REMOVE BONES AND SCALES FROM COD AND SIMMER FOR 10 MINUTES IN FISH STOCK (OR LIGHTLY SALTED WATER).

STIR IN COD (IN BITE-SIZE PIECES), LIQUID, POTATOES, CAPSICUM, PEPPER AND BACON/ONION MIXTURE.

BRING TO BOIL.

COVER AND SIMMER UNTIL POTATOES ARE TENDER.

STIR IN MILK THEN HEAT, STIRRING OCCASIONALLY, UNTIL HOT.

DO NOT BOIL.

GARNISH WITH PAPRIKA, CHIVES OR PARSLEY.

ADD TURMERIC.

SERVE WITH CRUSTY BREAD.

FISHING CAN BE FUN

KOSCIUSZKO WITH ORANGE SKY
PRAWN MYSTERY

SERVES 4

IT'S OK FOR YOU CRUISING THROUGH THIS LITTLE COOKBOOK. YOU CAN PUT IT DOWN WHEN YOU LIKE.

I'M THE ONE WHO HAS TO DO THE BLOODY WRITING. SITTING HERE, NOTHING TO EAT AND I'VE NAMED THIS BLOODY RECIPE KOSCIUSZKO WITH ORANGE SKY AND IT'S A PRAWN RECIPE.

BUT THE EDITOR'S A SNIVELLING DRUNK... HE PROBABLY WON'T EVEN NOTICE THIS UNMITIGATED CRAP. SO IF YOU'RE READING THIS, HE HASN'T.

½ TEASPOON CHOPPED DILL

4 SLICES BREAD, BUTTERED

50g/2oz EMMENTHAL CHEESE, GRATED

3 DESSERTSPOONS CREAM

3 TABLESPOONS MAYONNAISE

250g/9oz SMALL PRAWNS, COOKED AND PEELED

PLACE BREAD, BUTTERED SIDE DOWN, ON BAKING TRAY.

COMBINE CHEESE, CREAM, DILL AND MAYONNAISE IN A BOWL.

SEASON.

ADD PRAWNS, RESERVING A FEW FOR GARNISH.

SPREAD MIXTURE ON TOP OF BREAD.

TOP WITH STIFFLY BEATEN EGG WHITES.

BAKE IN PREHEATED OVEN AT 220°C/425°F/GAS MARK 7 UNTIL WELL RISEN AND BROWNED (ABOUT 10-15 MINUTES).

SERVE IMMEDIATELY AS AN EASY LUNCH OR A SPECTACULAR BREAKFAST.

GREEN FISH JUMPING
WARM BALSAMIC FISH SALAD

SERVES 4

2 TEASPOONS OLIVE OIL

500g/1lb TUNA FILLETS (OR ATLANTIC SALMON) CUT IN 3cm CUBES

8 FRESH ASPARAGUS SPEARS, HALVED

ABOUT 4 LARGE HANDFULS OF ROCKET

12 CHERRY TOMATOES, QUARTERED

1 LEBANESE CUCUMBER SALAD

HEAT OIL IN NON-STICK PAN.

COOK FISH ON HIGH HEAT UNTIL BROWNED ON BOTH SIDES AND FLESH JUST FLAKES.

BOIL ASPARAGUS AND RINSE UNDER COLD WATER.

ARRANGE ROCKET, TOMATOES, ASPARAGUS AND CUCUMBER IN SERVING BOWL.

TOP WITH HOT FISH.

DRIZZLE WITH BALSAMIC DRESSING.

SERVE WITH CRUSTY BREAD.

BALSAMIC DRESSING:

80ml/⅓ CUP BALSAMIC VINEGAR
2 TABLESPOONS LEMON OR LIME JUICE
2 TEASPOONS DIJON MUSTARD
FRESHLY GROUND BLACK PEPPER
2 TEASPOONS VIRGIN OLIVE OIL

COMBINE IN A SCREW-TOP CONTAINER AND SHAKE.

THIS IS NOT A GREEN FISH
AND IT'S NOT JUMPING.
BUT WHAT CAN YOU
EXPECT FROM AN
INEXPENSIVE BOOK

PINK SEA RISING
FISH STEW

SERVES 4

½ CAPSICUM, FINELY CHOPPED
1 LARGE ONION, PEELED AND CHOPPED
1 TABLESPOON OLIVE OIL
1 MEDIUM CAN TOMATOES
2 TABLESPOONS CHOPPED PARSLEY
½ TEASPOON CAYENNE PEPPER
100g/4oz ZUCCHINI/COURGETTE
4 FILLETS OCEAN PERCH (OR SO) - CHOPPED IN 2CM CUBES
SALT AND PEPPER

SAUTE ONION LIGHTLY IN OLIVE OIL FOR 2-3 MINUTES.

ADD TOMATOES, PARSLEY, CAPSICUM, CAYENNE, SALT AND PEPPER.

STIR WELL, BRING TO BOIL AND COOK 2-3 MINUTES.

ADD ZUCCHINI AND FISH, RETURN TO BOIL, COVER AND SIMMER UNTIL FISH IS COOKED.

SERVE OVER RICE.

VARIATIONS ARE ENDLESS, JUST CHANGE THE VEGETABLES.

CYCLONE ERNIE
FISH PARCELS

SERVES 4

I WAS EATING FISH PARCELS ON AN ISLAND IN THE MIDDLE OF ERAKOR LAGOON IN VANUATU, WHICH IS LIKE GOING BACK TO 1950. TOMORROW THEY COULD SHOOT MCHALE'S NAVY THERE WITHOUT BUILDING A SET.

WHILE MOST OF THE OTHER RESORTS AND TOWNS IN THE PACIFIC HAVE AN ARCHITECTURAL STYLE CALLED CRAPPOLA MODERNE, VANUATU HAS AN AWARD-WINNING STYLE CALLED HAVEN'T CHANGED A THING. TEN OUT OF TEN.

BUT THE NATIVES WERE LOOKING NERVOUS AS LIGHTNING FLASHED OVER THE HORIZON.

I HAD BEEN LISTENING TO THE RADIO FOR TWO DAYS. THERE ARE TWO RADIO STATIONS IN VANUATU. ONE IS FRENCH SPOKEN AT MACHINE-GUN SPEED. THE OTHER IS PIDGIN. THE TWO RADIO STATIONS COME ON AIR AT RANDOM AND APPARENTLY UNANNOUNCED TIMES.

I KNOW ONLY ONE PHRASE OF PIDGIN. IN ENGLISH IT SAYS, WHAT TIME BIG BIRD FALL DOWN OUT OF SKY? WHICH IS THE MAKE-YOUR-KNEES-SHAKE VERSION OF, WHAT TIME DOES THE FLIGHT ARRIVE?

OVER TWO DAYS I HAD DISCOVERED THAT THERE MIGHT BE TWO CYCLONES NEARBY, IN PIDGIN, FRENCH AND AMAZING STATIC.

ONE MAY HAVE BEEN A THOUSAND KILOMETRES TO THE EAST AND THE OTHER A THOUSAND KILOMETRES TO THE WEST. MAYBE.

THE WEATHER WAS BRIGHT BUT IT WAS NIGHT.
THE SURF ON THE OUTER REEF WAS ROARING LIKE THOUSANDS OF TIGERS.

THE OUTDOOR ISLAND CAFE I WAS EATING AT WAS ABOUT SIX FEET ABOVE SEA LEVEL. BUT SALT WATER WAS POURING INTO MY SHOES.

IN THE MESS OF PIDGIN AND FRENCH PLUS STATIC. I THOUGHT THAT ONE OF THE CYCLONES WAS CALLED ERNIE. IF I WAS RIGHT, ERNIE WAS COMING TO GET ME.

SO I DRANK HEAVILY AND SLEPT SIMILARLY. IN THE MORNING THE WEATHER WAS PERFECT.
IN MEMORY OF FISH PARCELS AND THAT FEARFUL NIGHT I NAME THIS DISH CYCLONE ERNIE.

PIDGIN

4 OILY OR WHITE FISH CUTLETS
125ml/½ CUP COCONUT MILK
2 TABLESPOONS SOY SAUCE
2 CLOVES GARLIC, CHOPPED
2 RED CHILLIES, CHOPPED
40g/⅓ CUP SHALLOTS, CHOPPED
½ TEASPOON CUMIN
½ TEASPOON CORIANDER
¼ TEASPOON TURMERIC

PREHEAT OVEN TO 200°C/400°F/GAS MARK 6.
COMBINE COCONUT MILK, SOY SAUCE, GARLIC, CHILLIES,
SHALLOTS, CUMIN, CORIANDER AND TURMERIC.
MIX WELL.
PLACE 4 SHEETS OF FOIL ON BENCH, 1 FILLET ON EACH.
RAISE SIDES OF FOIL.
POUR ¼ OF COCONUT MILK MIXTURE ON EACH.
FOLD FOIL TO ENCLOSE FISH AND JUICES, FORMING
SMALL PARCELS.
BAKE FOR 10 MINUTES ON BAKING TRAY (OR UNTIL
TENDER). SERVE WITH STEAMED RICE

WARM DARWIN DAYS
TANGY FISH FILLETS

SERVES 4

4 200g/7oz FISH FILLETS (HAKE OR SIMILAR)
100g/½ CUP MAYONNAISE
1 TABLESPOON CAPERS
1 TABLESPOON PICKLED CUCUMBERS
1 TABLESPOON CORIANDER OR DILL
60g/½ CUP CHEDDAR CHEESE, GRATED
HANDFUL OF BREADCRUMBS
2 DESSERTSPOONS BUTTER
LEMON OR ORANGE ZEST TO GARNISH

PAT FISH FILLETS DRY. PLACE INTO FOIL-LINED GRILL PAN. SEASON WITH SALT AND FRESHLY GROUND BLACK PEPPER.

IN A BOWL, COMBINE MAYONNAISE, CAPERS, PICKLED CUCUMBERS, CORIANDER AND SPREAD OVER FILLETS.

IN ANOTHER BOWL, COMBINE CHEESE AND BREADCRUMBS. SPRINKLE OVER FILLETS, DOT WITH BUTTER AND SEASON.

GRILL UNTIL GOLDEN AND CRISPY - ABOUT 10 MINUTES, DEPENDING ON THICKNESS.

GARNISH WITH LEMON OR ORANGE ZEST AND SERVE WITH SALAD AND RICE, OR MAYBE BAKED POTATOES.

BLUE PACIFIC NOON
GRILLED ATLANTIC SALMON CUTLETS

SERVES 6

SPLASH OF DRY VERMOUTH
6 ATLANTIC SALMON CUTLETS
4 TABLESPOONS BUTTER, MELTED
1 TEASPOON FRESH LEMON THYME
1 TEASPOON PEPPER
1 LEMON, THINLY SLICED
LEMON THYME FOR GARNISH

BRUSH FISH WITH MELTED BUTTER ON BAKING DISH.

SPRINKLE WITH LEMON THYME AND SEASON.

ARRANGE LEMON SLICES ON TOP, SPLASH WITH VERMOUTH.

WRAP FOIL LOOSELY AROUND THE FISH.

GRILL FOR 10-15 MINUTES OR UNTIL FISH FLAKES WHEN TOUCHED WITH FORK.

REMOVE FOIL.

GARNISH WITH LEMON THYME.

SERVE WITH SEASONAL VEGETABLES.

BUTTERNUT BLUE
CRISPY PRAWN SALAD

SERVES 6

1 BUTTERNUT PUMPKIN, PEELED
3 MEDIUM BEETROOTS, PEELED
2 SWEET POTATOES, PEELED
30 PRAWNS, SHELLED, DEVEINED AND CLEANED
OIL FOR FRYING

MARINADE:
1 TEASPOON ROOT GINGER, FINELY GRATED
2 TABLESPOONS TOASTED SESAME OIL
3 TEASPOONS OYSTER SAUCE
3 TEASPOONS SOY SAUCE
60ml/¼ CUP ORANGE JUICE

SLICE THE BUTTERNUT, BEETROOT AND SWEET POTATO INTO 1CM SLICES.
MIX GINGER WITH 15ML OF SESAME OIL, SOY SAUCE, OYSTER SAUCE AND ORANGE JUICE.
MARINATE PRAWNS FOR 30 MINUTES.
HEAT OIL IN DEEP PAN. FRY BUTTERNUT, BEETROOT AND

SWEET POTATO SLICES SEPARATELY IN BATCHES UNTIL
CRISP.

DRAIN ON ABSORBENT PAPER.

HEAT REMAINING SESAME OIL AND FRY PRAWNS, POUR
IN THE MARINADE AND BRING TO THE BOIL.

ARRANGE BUTTERNUT, BEETROOT AND SWEET POTATO
CHIPS ONTO SERVING PLATES.

SPOON 5 PRAWNS PER SERVING AND A LITTLE MARINADE
OVER THE CHIPS.

SERVE IMMEDIATELY WITH SALAD.

VARIATION: TRY PARSNIP CHIPS.

MANGO MANGO
SMOKED SALMON, AVOCADO AND MANGO SALAD

SERVES 4

1 AVOCADO, CUT INTO SLICES
16 SLICES SMOKED SALMON
1 MANGO, CUT INTO STRIPS
75g/½ CUP CROUTONS
60g/½ CUP WALNUTS, HALVED
ASSORTED SALAD LEAVES, WASHED

ARRANGE LETTUCE LEAVES ON INDIVIDUAL PLATES.
ARRANGE SALMON, AVOCADO AND MANGO ON TOP.
GARNISH WITH CROUTONS AND WALNUTS.
POUR DILL MAYONNAISE OVER.

DILL MAYONNAISE:
2 TABLESPOONS WHITE WINE VINEGAR
1 TEASPOON CASTOR SUGAR
1 TEASPOON SEED MUSTARD
4 TEASPOONS OLIVE OIL
1 TEASPOON DILL, CHOPPED
PINCH OF SALT

WHISK TOGETHER VINEGAR, SALT AND SUGAR UNTIL
DISSOLVED.
SLOWLY WHISK IN MUSTARD AND OLIVE OIL UNTIL WELL
MIXED.
ADD THE DILL AND POUR OVER SALAD.

POST-MODERN MANGO

FREE CHILLI
STEAMED FISH

SERVES 4

I WAS IN A CELL WITH PABLO NERUDA IN THE DARK
DAYS OF REVOLUTION.

HE WROTE BEAUTIFUL POEMS ON THE DIM CREAM
WALLS WITH CHARCOAL FROM AN OPEN FIRE THAT
WAS NEVER LIT.

SIXTY DAYS AND SIXTY NIGHTS. THEN THE SOUND
OF GUNSHOTS IN THE STREETS. THE SOUND
OF RUNNING FOOTSTEPS DOWN THE STONE
CORRIDORS.

WOULD THEY BRING FREEDOM... OR WOULD THEY
BRING A BULLET. THEY BROUGHT NEITHER.

THEY BROUGHT STEAMED FISH WITH CHILLI AND
FRAGRANT HERBS. AND THEY BROUGHT FREEDOM.
ALL I CAN BRING YOU IS THE RECIPE.

UNEXPECTED HOWLING DOG

800g/¾lb SNAPPER, IN BITE-SIZED PIECES

2 TABLESPOONS VEGETABLE OIL

2 TABLESPOONS CHOPPED GARLIC

250ml/1 CUP LIME JUICE

6 TABLESPOONS THAI FISH SAUCE

PINCH SALT

2 TABLESPOONS EACH OF CHOPPED CORIANDER, BASIL, GINGER, LEMONGRASS, SPRING ONIONS

8 FRESH KAFFIR LIME LEAVES, ROUGHLY CHOPPED

2 TABLESPOONS CHOPPED RED CHILLIES

MARINATE SNAPPER IN OIL AND 1 TABLESPOON OF THAI FISH SAUCE FOR 10 MINUTES.

STEAM FISH UNTIL COOKED.

COMBINE ALL OTHER INGREDIENTS IN A BOWL.

ARRANGE FISH ON PLATTER.

POUR OVER SAUCE AND SERVE.

CHINATOWN CUTLETS
ORIENTAL TUNA

SERVES 4

4 TUNA CUTLETS
60ml/¼ CUP FRESH ORANGE JUICE
60ml/¼ CUP SOY SAUCE
60ml/¼ CUP OYSTER SAUCE
2 TABLESPOONS CHOPPED PARSLEY
1 TABLESPOON LEMON JUICE
1 TEASPOON GRATED LEMON RIND
1 CLOVE OR GARLIC, CRUSHED
1 TEASPOON GARAM MASALA

COMBINE ALL INGREDIENTS IN A SHALLOW DISH.

MARINATE TUNA CUTLETS IN THIS MIXTURE FOR 3 HOURS.
GRILL CUTLETS FOR ABOUT 3 MINUTES EACH SIDE,

BASTING WITH MARINADE DURING COOKING.

SERVE WITH GREEN SALAD TOSSED IN LEMON JUICE AND
HONEY.

PRINCESS'S TAKEAWAY
SALMON AND CAVIAR PIZZA

SERVES 2

LOGOS BEGAN WHEN MURDEROUS THUGS IN DISTANT CENTURIES BECAME SUCCESSFUL ENOUGH TO HAVE PERSONAL LOGOS WHICH WERE THEN CALLED HERALDRY. HERALDRY CAUSED CONSIDERABLE EXCITEMENT AND QUICKLY LEAD TO PAGEANTRY.

PAGEANTRY WAS BASED ON THE ABILITY TO RUN POPULAR EVENTS AND HAVE YOUR LOGO HELD ALOFT ON BIG STICKS.

OVER THE YEARS, WITH THE HELP OF HERALDRY AND PAGEANTRY, THE DESCENDANTS OF THE MOST SUCCESSFUL OF THE PSYCHOPATHS BECAME KNOWN AS ROYALTY.

THIS THEN LED TO THE ESTABLISHMENT OF CORPORATE HEADQUARTERS WHICH WERE KNOWN AS PALACES.

IF THE PALACES WERE USING TOTAL QUALITY MANAGEMENT, THEN THE MEALS WERE SERVED ON TIME AND THE HORSES WERE GROOMED PROPERLY. ALL OF THIS MEANT THAT THE PALACES OF ROYALTY GREW LARGER AS THE CHINS OF ROYALTY GREW SMALLER.

BUT WHAT OF THE POOR PEOPLE WHO DIDN'T HAVE LOGOS? WELL, THEY DID IN A SENSE. IN RETURN FOR OBEDIENCE, THEY WERE GRANTED ILLITERACY.

THROUGH ILLITERACY THEY GOT LOGOS, GIVEN TO THEM SO THAT TRADE COULD BECOME SIMPLER.

THE POOR PEOPLE DRANK BEER AND ATE PIZZA.

IF THE PUBLICAN PAINTED THE WORD 'BEER' ON HIS SIGN IT DIDN'T MEAN MUCH TO THEM BECAUSE THEY COULDN'T READ. FOR ALL THEY KNEW IT MIGHT SAY, ENROL HERE FOR A LIFE IN THE ARMY.

IT JUST WASN'T WORTH TAKING THE RISK.
BUT IF THE PUBLICAN PAINTED A BIG FOAMING JUG OF BEER ON HIS SIGN HE'S GOT YOU. HE'S GOT ME, ANYWAY. WELCOME TO THE POOR PEOPLE'S FIRST LOGO.

THE SAME APPLIED TO TAKEAWAY FOOD. SO TO MAKE UP FOR ALL THE CRAP FOOD YOU ATE IN THE 13TH CENTURY, HERE'S A PIZZA FIT FOR A PRINCESS.

IS ANY OF THIS MAKING SENSE?

NO WONDER BILLY JOE MACALLISTER JUMPED OFF THE TALLAHASSEE BRIDGE.

2 VERY THIN, COOKED PIZZA BASES

125ml/½ CUP FRESH TOMATO SAUCE (OR USE TOMATO PUREE)

80ml/⅓ CUP SOUR CREAM

200g/7oz SMOKED SALMON

4 TABLESPOONS CAVIAR

1 TABLESPOON CHOPPED DILL

SPREAD TOMATO SAUCE OVER BASES.

COVER WITH SOUR CREAM.

LAYER THE SMOKED SALMON OVER THE CREAM.

SPREAD CAVIAR ON TOP.

COOK AT 200°C/400°F/GAS MARK 6 UNTIL HOT (ABOUT 10 MINUTES), SPRINKLE WITH CHOPPED DILL.

SERVE WITH A GREEN SALAD.

THURSDAY'S BREAKFAST
STEAMED CRAB

THIS IS NOT A LIE.

ONCE UPON A TIME, I WAS MAROONED AT A BEACH DURING A HUGE STORM.

I HAD DRIVEN 40KM DOWN A FIRE TRAIL IN AN OLD VOLKSWAGEN. IN THE SAME FEW HOURS I ARRIVED AT THE BEACH, MY BATTERY WENT FLAT AND THE HINTERLAND BEHIND THE BEACH BECAME FLOODED. I WAS STRANDED FOR FORTY DAYS AND NEVER SAW A HUMAN BEING.

I HAD NO FISHING LINES BUT I DID HAVE UNDERWATER GOGGLES. ABOUT 100 METRES OFF THE BEACH WAS A REEF. IT WAS COVERED IN LOBSTERS. I COULD SWIM OUT AND GRAB ONE IN EACH HAND AND LIE ON MY BACK AND KICK MY WAY TO THE BEACH. THE LOBSTERS THEN MADE CLICKING NOISES THAT I BELIEVE SHARKS ARE PLEASED TO HEAR.

BEHIND THE BEACH WERE GROVES OF BANANA TREES. I COOKED THE LOBSTER IN MY VOLKSWAGEN'S HUB CAPS. THEN I HAD LOBSTER AND BANANA DAY AFTER DAY, MEAL AFTER MEAL. ONE DAY I CAUGHT A CRAB THAT WAS SO GIGANTIC, I THOUGHT THAT IT MIGHT MAIM ME. BUT I WON THE BATTLE AND ATE IT FOR BREAKFAST. CRAB AND BANANAS. I THINK IT WAS A THURSDAY.

1 LEMON, SLICED
500ml/2 CUPS WATER
500ml/2 CUPS WHITE VINEGAR
FRESH CRABS (1 PER PERSON, DEPENDS ON SIZE)
1 TABLESPOON DRY MUSTARD
1 TEASPOON PAPRIKA

PUT WATER, WINE VINEGAR AND SLICED LEMON INTO BASE OF STEAMER.

SPRINKLE CRABS WITH MUSTARD AND PAPRIKA AND PLACE IN TOP HALF OF STEAMER.

CLOSE TIGHTLY AND STEAM OVER MODERATE HEAT UNTIL COOKED (ABOUT 15 MINUTES, DEPENDING ON SIZE0.

WARATAH STREET HIDEOUT
TUNA AND SPAGHETTI

SPAGHETTI

CANS OF TUNA, ONE VERY SMALL CAN PER PERSON

SEVERAL CLOVES OF GARLIC

BUTTER

CHOPPED PARSLEY

SLICE GARLIC CLOVES UP INTO SMALL PIECES.

PUT SOME BUTTER INTO A PAN AND FOLLOW WITH GARLIC AND CHOPPED PARSLEY.

TOAST IT AS BROWN OR BLACK AS YOU LIKE.

PUT SPAGHETTI INTO BOILING WATER.

WHEN COOKED, DRAIN.

PUT SPAGHETTI INTO INDIVIDUAL BOWLS.

PUT TUNA ON TOP OF SPAGHETTI.

POUR GARLIC MIX ON TOP OF TUNA AND SPAGHETTI.

SERVE WITH A SIMPLE SIDE SALAD.

MANGO WATERFALL
REDFISH WITH MANGO

SERVES 4

4 REDFISH FILLETS
125ml/½ CUP DRY WHITE WINE
½ TEASPOON GROUND BAY LEAVES
1 MANGO, PEELED AND SLICED
660g/4 CUPS HOT, COOKED
LONG-GRAIN RICE.

POACH FILLETS IN WINE UNTIL THEY FLAKE WHEN TOUCHED WITH FORK.

REMOVE TO SERVING PLATTER AND KEEP WARM.

ADD BAY LEAVES AND MANGO TO WINE. SIMMER FOR 3 MINUTES, REMOVE BAY LEAVES.

ARRANGE MANGO ON TOP OF THE FISH.

POUR SAUCE OVER.

SERVE WITH RICE.

RED BUTTERFLY
MUSTARD PRAWNS

SERVES 4

1kg/2lb LARGE GREEN PRAWNS, GUTTED, CLEANED AND HEADED

150g/5oz BUTTER

1 TABLESPOON OLIVE OIL

1 TABLESPOON FINELY CHOPPED ONION

½ TEASPOON CHOPPED GARLIC

1 TEASPOON DIJON MUSTARD

1 TEASPOON CHOPPED FRESH HERBS (TARRAGON OR PARSLEY)

125ml/½ CUP BRANDY

125ml/½ CUP CREAM

FRESHLY GROUND BLACK PEPPER

SALT IF NEEDED

CUT CLEANED PRAWNS DOWN CENTRE AND OPEN OUT BUTTERFLY-STYLE, LEAVING TAIL INTACT.

MELT HALF THE BUTTER IN A DEEP PAN.

ADD PRAWNS, ONION, GARLIC, MUSTARD, HERBS, PEPPER AND SALT.

COOK OVER MEDIUM HEAT FOR 8-10 MINUTES, ACCORDING TO THE SIZE OF PRAWNS.

ADD BRANDY TO PAN. THEN FLAME.

ADD CREAM, THEN THICKEN WITH REMAINING BUTTER. SERVE ON HOT PLATES IMMEDIATELY WITH SALAD AND WILD RICE.

COOK IT AGAIN SAM
MOROCCAN FISH

SERVES 4-6

I WAS IN MOROCCO ONCE. I LOVED IT.

VERY, VERY EXCITING PLACE IF YOU DIDN'T STAY AT THE HILTON.

A FINE PLACE TO DRINK FOUR BLOCKS BACK FROM THE TOURISTS.

BUT WHEN THEY STAMPED MY PASSPORT ON THE WAY OUT, I FELT VERY RELIEVED THAT I HADN'T OFFENDED ANYONE IN SOME OF THE BARS FIVE BLOCKS BACK.

6 WHITE FISH CUTLETS
2 ONIONS, SLICED
5 TABLESPOONS OLIVE OIL
250ml/1 CUP TOMATO PASTE
6 OLIVES (OR SO)
1 TABLESPOON CHOPPED PARSLEY
SALT AND PEPPER
FRESH CHOPPED CORIANDER

PUT SLICED ONIONS ONTO HEATPROOF DISH, TOP WITH FRESH CORIANDER.

PLACE FISH FILLETS ON TOP.

ADD OIL AND TOMATO PASTE AND POUR WATER OVER FISH UNTIL IT IS JUST COVERED.

ADD OLIVES, PARSLEY, SALT AND PEPPER.

BAKE IN MODERATE OVEN FOR 45 MINUTES.

SERVE WITH COUSCOUS AND GREEN SALAD.

THIS AEROPLANE IS AN OBSCURE REFERENCE
TO THE LAST SCENE IN CASABLANCA

JAMAICA RAFT
CREOLE FILLETS

SERVES 6

3 TABLESPOONS OLIVE OIL

2 MEDIUM ONIONS, PEELED AND SLICED

1 GREEN PEPPER, SEEDED AND SLICED

1 STALK OF CELERY, CHOPPED

½ TEASPOON CHILLI POWDER (OR TO TASTE)

SALT

FRESHLY GROUND BLACK PEPPER

1kg/2lb WHITE FISH FILLETS, CUBED

1 410g/14oz CAN WHOLE TOMATOES, CHOPPED

2 TABLESPOONS TOMATO PUREE

1 DESSERTSPOON BROWN SUGAR

SAUTE ONIONS, GREEN AND RED PEPPERS AND CELERY UNTIL TENDER.

ADD CHILLI POWDER, SALT, PEPPER AND FISH.

STIR MIXTURE TOGETHER.

POUR TOMATO, TOMATO PUREE AND SUGAR INTO SAUCEPAN.

SIMMER GENTLY UNTIL FISH IS COOKED THROUGH.

SERVE WITH RICE.

JAILHOUSE FILLET
DORY FILLETS WITH AVOCADO MACADAMIA CREAM

SERVES 4

1 RIPE AVOCADO, PEELED, SEEDED AND CUT INTO CHUNKS

30g/¼ CUP ROASTED MACADAMIA NUTS, SKINNED

125g/½ CUP SOFT CREAM CHEESE

2 TABLESPOONS LEMON JUICE

2 TABLESPOONS BUTTER

MIX AVOCADO, MACADEMIA NUTS, CREAM CHEESE AND LEMON JUICE IN BLENDER UNTIL SMOOTH.

MELT BUTTER IN FRYING PAN.

PUT SEVERAL DORY FILLETS IN PAN AT A TIME.

COVER WITH AVOCADO CREAM.

GENTLY POACH FOR 6-8 MINUTES OR UNTIL FLESH FLAKES.

SERVE WITH BOILED NEW POTATOES AND GREEN BEANS.

SLARKI YARKI
TERIYAKI KINGFISH

SERVES 2

2 KINGFISH FILLETS

1 TEASPOON FRESH GRATED GINGER

1 TABLESPOON SOY SAUCE

1 TABLESPOON MIRIN (RICE VINEGAR) OR SWEET SHERRY

LEMON JUICE OR FRESHLY GRATED HORSERADISH

MARINATE WHOLE FILLETS IN SOY SAUCE, MIRIN AND GINGER FOR 1-2 HOURS.

THREAD EACH FILLET ONTO TWO PARALLEL SKEWERS TO KEEP FIRM AND GRILL UNTIL COOKED.
(SOAK SKEWERS IN COLD WATER FIRST TO PREVENT THEM FROM BURNING).

SERVE WITH LEMON JUICE OR HORSERADISH.

ET TU BANANA
BANANA OR MANGO FILLETS

SERVES 4-6

4-6 FILLETS OF WHITE FISH (LING, FLAKE, OCEAN PERCH)
1 CAN COCONUT MILK
2 BANANAS, SLICED
OR
2 MANGOES, SLICED
1 TEASPOON CURRY POWDER
½ TEASPOON CUMIN
FRESHLY GROUND BLACK PEPPER
½ TEASPOON GARAM MASALA

PUT LAYERS OF FISH AND FRUIT IN OVENPROOF DISH.

MIX SPICES WITH COCONUT MILK.

POUR OVER FISH AND FRUIT.

BAKE AT 180°C/350°F/GAS MARK 4 FOR 30 MINUTES.

SERVE WITH GREEN SALAD AND BAKED POTATOES.

YELLOW BUTTERFLY
PASTA WITH SALMON

SERVES 3-4

1 200g/7oz CAN SALMON IN OIL
400g/14oz PASTA (VARY THE TYPE YOU USE)
150g/5oz MUSHROOMS
1 CLOVE GARLIC, CHOPPED
1 TEASPOON CAPERS, CHOPPED
1 TOMATO, DICED
60ml/¼ CUP DRY WHITE WINE
FRESHLY GROUND BLACK PEPPER
1 TABLESPOON GRATED PARMESAN CHEESE

STRAIN SALMON AND SAVE OIL.

BOIL LARGE POT OF SALTED WATER AND COOK PASTA.

SLICE WASHED MUSHROOMS.

HEAT SALMON OIL IN SAUCEPAN AND GENTLY FRY GARLIC AND CAPERS FOR A FEW SECONDS.

ADD MUSHROOMS. STIR-FRY FOR A MINUTE.

ADD TOMATO AND COOK 3-4 MINUTES, ADD WINE.

CRUMBLE SALMON INTO PAN AND SEASON.

POUR OVER PASTA AND MIX THROUGH.
SPRINKLE WITH PARMESAN CHEESE AND PEPPER AND SERVE.

IT'S A LUNCH OR A SIMPLE SUPPER.

SOUGHING SEA
CEVICHE

SERVES 4-6

**500g/1lb FIRM WHITE FISH FILLETS
(SNAPPER, DORY, BREAM)
1 TEASPOON SALT
60ml/¼ CUP LEMON OR LIME JUICE
1 MEDIUM ONION, FINELY CHOPPED
60ml/¼ CUP COCONUT MILK
1 GREEN PEPPER, FINELY CHOPPED
IN SLIVERS
6 CHERRY TOMATOES, HALVED
1 CHILLI, SLICED, SEEDED**

CUT FISH INTO BITE-SIZED PIECES.

SPRINKLE WITH SALT, LEMON JUICE AND CHILLI.

COVER AND CHILL FOR 2 HOURS OR UNTIL FISH WHITENS,
STIRRING OCCASIONALLY.

DRAIN.

STIR IN ONION, GREEN PEPPER AND COCONUT MILK.

PUT TOMATOES ON TOP.

SERVE CHILLED.

A GREAT SUMMER ENTREE OR ACCOMPANIMENT
TO SALADS.

COOKING FISH

POACHING

JUST COVER THE FISH IN LIQUID (WATER AND/OR WINE, STOCK, MILK, BEER, VINEGAR, LEMON JUICE)

ADD ONION, PEPPERCORNS, A BAY LEAF.

COOK GENTLY BELOW BOILING POINT, 8-15 MINUTES, DEPENDING ON SIZE.

LEAVE IN POACHING LIQUID IF DISH IS TO BE SERVED COLD, SO IT STAYS MOIST.

GOOD FOR LING, SNAPPER, PERCH, WHOLE WHITING, DORY, CORAL TROUT.

BAKING

IF WHOLE, YOU MAY WISH TO STUFF IT FIRST (TRY COOKED RICE, GRATED LEMON RIND AND SAUTEED MUSHROOMS).

GREASE BAKING DISH AND PUT FISH IN.

ADD SEASONING AND LIQUID (TOMATO OR LEMON JUICE, WINE, HONEY AND SOY, ETC).

BRUSH FISH WITH OIL, PEPPER AND SALT.

COVER DISH ROUGHLY WITH FOIL AND BAKE AT 180°C/350°F/GAS MARK 4 UNTIL DONE (TIME DEPENDS ON SIZE).

PAN FRYING

GOOD FOR SMALL FILLETS (WHITING, DORY, SILVER BREAM).

USE A MIXTURE OF OIL AND BUTTER, OR GHEE. COOK FOR 3-5 MINUTES ACCORDING TO SIZE, UNTIL GOLDEN AND FLAKY.

STEAMING

USE FIRM MOIST FISH LIKE SNAPPER, GEMFISH, LING.

STEAM OVER BOILING WATER UNTIL FLESH FLAKES.

MAY BE WRAPPED IN FOIL.

GRILLING

BRUSH FISH WITH MELTED BUTTER, LEMON JUICE OR WHITE WINE (TO PREVENT DRYING OUT).

SCORE THICK FISH DIAGONALLY 2 OR 3 TIMES ON OUTER SKIN FOR EVEN COOKING.

PLACE UNDER HEATED GRILL (ON MODERATE HEAT).

BASTE **AGAIN** DURING COOKING AND TURN ONCE.

GOOD FOR MULLET, TAILOR, LING, PERCH, SOLE, BREAM.

BARBECUING

ALLOW FIRE TO BURN DOWN TO EMBERS (NO FLAMES).

BRUSH BARBECUE GRILL WITH OIL FIRST.

BASTE FISH WITH OIL, OR OIL AND BUTTER MIX, OR LEMON JUICE (OR BE INVENTIVE).

OR **WRAP** IN FOIL.
WHOLE FISH OR FILLETS, THEY CAN ALL BE BARBECUED.

ALWAYS READ **ALL THE RECIPE**
BEFORE YOU START.
ALWAYS MAKE SURE YOU HAVE **ALL THE INGREDIENTS** BEFORE YOU START.

FISH & CRUSTACEAN IDENTIFICATION

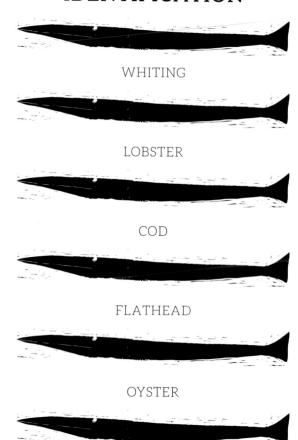

WHITING

LOBSTER

COD

FLATHEAD

OYSTER

BLUE SWIMMER CRAB

FISH & CRUSTACEAN
IDENTIFICATION

SALMON

BREAM

PRAWN

TUNA

CAVIAR

REDFISH

FISH & CRUSTACEAN IDENTIFICATION

SNAPPER

GEMFISH

LING

KEVIN

CECILIA

MULLET

FISH & CRUSTACEAN IDENTIFICATION

PERCH

SOLE

HEEL

SOUL

ELVIS

CORAL TROUT